So You Say
You Want To Teach

Marcus Strother

This book is for all those teachers that work tirelessly for our students. Who accept being more than just a teacher, and who understand that students truly don't care what you know, if they don't know that you care!

To my wife and children who deal with my immediate and in the moment ideas that keep me away from them. Your sacrifice is so much more than just letting me be me, it's sharing your time with those who need it!

To my mother and father, who blessed me with the strength to accept who I am!

To my students, all of you have made such a difference in my life. Thank you for allowing me to be a part of who you are. Thank you for allowing me to share my thoughts and ideas. This book is because of you, and how you taught me to be a better me!

Contents

Introduction

As a more than 10-year veteran in education, I have experienced many different situations that have contributed to the writing of this book. I also know that there are more than "10 things" an educator will experience that they won't learn in college, so I am not attempting to qualify these "10 things" as the "10 things" you won't learn, but they have been the 10 most important experiences that have contributed to my success as an educator. I have worked with some of the most talented educators in the world and I have experienced some of the worst. I have been taught how to educate by both as well, and those lessons were equally valuable.

As a young student, I experienced an educator that taught me exactly what I believed a good educator was. This teacher was a mentor, at times a parent, and as our relationship grew, this teacher became someone I called friend. I still have that relationship with this teacher today, as you read this book.

I also experienced a teacher who taught me everything that I did not want to be as an educator. I can remember my first day in her class with her asking me this question. "What's it like being black and having a white mother?" Now to clarify, I am bi-racial and therefore my mother is Caucasian and my father is African-American, and I take it she thought this question would be appropriate. As the school year moved along, she realized that her question was indefinitely the wrong question. I made her life a living hell for the entire school year, because she chose to ask me that question. I disliked her for that one reason and she was never able to build a relationship with me, nor was I willing to allow her too. I actually began teaching in the same building as her later in life, and she just continued her inappropriate comments. Our first encounter as now colleagues was her saying to me, "I hope you get students just like you!" She had the biggest smile on her face saying this to me as if she was getting me back. I felt sorry for her because she had not yet learned what it meant to build a relationship and she held on to this for so long. I was 12 years removed from her class, and she still had that bad taste in her mouth for a young man that she probably considered an "at-risk" student, not knowing that I loved school, just hated her class! Sadly, we have never been able to rectify our relationship and she has since retired, but how many of our students have these experiences. Luckily, I let it only effect me for that year, but I could have easily turned off school from that point on.

My encounter with her as a student and later as a colleague helped me to become a better educator and to also write this book. I began writing this book to help those new and veteran teachers learn what those typical college courses won't teach. I wrote this book for the person who believes that just because they like working with kids, that they can teach. I wrote this book for the student who is being affected by the teacher who has not yet realized that this job is not an end of the workday career. On the front cover of this book is a character I created named Mr. Majestic! He was created to help all of us see that teacher that made a difference in our life. We have all had that one teacher that made us feel like we were the best at what we did. When you see Mr. Majestic, I hope that you see that teacher. He is featured in my children's book series entitled, "The Magical Teachings of Mr. Majestic." He is the teacher we all looked up to. He is the teacher that goes the extra mile. The teacher that keeps an extra box of granola bars in his desk because he knows that one of his students didn't eat last night. He is the teacher that tells you everyday that failure does not belong on you. He will not allow you the option of failing. We all know great teachers. I work very closely with many in my school. I am a part of a great Freedom Writer Teacher community and family, which is made up of many great teachers. There are great programs pushing out great teachers like Teach for America, and many of our universities and colleges are doing the same. We have also created some inconsistencies in the educators we have produced. I believe much of this is because many people have decided to become a teacher, not knowing that this profession is much more than knowing your subject area or how to do curriculum mapping. I hope this book will provide new and veteran educators, as well as those considering the profession an applicable insight into the world of education and what it means too be someone who teaches. Caring is job number one, not educating, because if you don't care about the students you encounter, they will know, and they will not learn from you. The students allow you to educate them, not you educating the students. That tip is free! Please read this book with the intent it is made and that is to help anyone in his or her decision to become an educator and to also help those already in the profession, to consider these lessons as a guide in your continued journey as an educator who is working to create opportunities and pass on HOPE!

Chapter 1

The Conversation

It's Christmas day and we were spending our time with family as many families do. There were Christmas toasts, good food, great gifts, and of course, a borage of conversations. I was spending my time with my second love, music. I was watching the Hall of Fame concert on HBO when a certain conversation caught my attention. This conversation was not unusual, nor was it unique. I have been a part of many of these conversations and have heard my share of them as well. A small group of the family was talking about what they were up to and how life was going. My nephew decided to share his current goals, and it was at that time that I became very interested. I care about him dearly, so it was good to hear that he had some goals and I wanted to know what they were. As he talked, I knew exactly where he was going because he made comments like; "I love working with kids," and "I want to do something that I will enjoy." I waited to hear that statement that I have heard from so many, but I wasn't sure that he truly understood what he could possibly be getting into, similar to many others. I sat and listened and it came out. "I think I want to teach." Even though this statement alone did not birth the idea of this book, it definitely was a huge help. Ethically, it is important for us as educators to be responsible for those future educators whom decide that teaching is their calling. It is utterly important that we share what really occurs in classrooms, and what it truly means to be a teacher, or what it truly means to teach. Teaching is much more important than just being a teacher by title and I will get into that later on. I encourage anyone that has found himself in the tug and pull of deciding if teaching is what he wants to do, to answer this simple question. "Do you want to teach or do you want to be a teacher?" As I listened to my nephew express his interest in teaching, I found it necessary for me to ask a question of my own. "Why do you want to teach?"

Chapter 2

<u>Work with a Purpose</u>

I've been told that I care too much. They've told me my heart is too big to do this job. I've had every reason to become the burnt out teacher and quit, but I have also had every reason to continue to wake up and do it all over again. When I started teaching over ten years ago, I began by thinking about what made a difference to me as a student who once sat in these same chairs. What made me want to perform? Don't get me wrong, I do not want to set you up and make you believe that I was the valedictorian of my class. I didn't even get to say that I was in the top fifty of my class, but I do know that I always did and still do love going to school. So I guess I was destined to become a teacher, since I enjoyed spending so much time there.

This journey has been one that has brought me to tears many times. I believe now that I am at a point where I can share that my tears have been more because of the joy that comes with this job, as opposed to the not so joyous occasions. When my wife said to me one evening that I should write about my experiences, my first thought was "Who else would want to hear these stories?" There are amazing teachers all over and I know many of them. I am a proud member of the Freedom Writer Teachers. I hear all of their stories of amazing accomplishments and know that there is great learning happening all over the world. Then a domino effect of amazing moments happened. Like many of the young men and women that I work with, we all have a story. I traveled with my Brother 2 Brother group to

Indianapolis to attend a conference and what occurred that late Friday night was one of the reasons that I knew that these stories needed to be shared. I watched nine young men break down all barriers. These young men left everything they had in room 408. As a great colleague and I, Dan Harris, began breaking down different sections of the day's events, the light turned on and stories began to flow.

One young man talked about his battle with his grandmother, another began talking about his relationship with his mother and why it has affected him so much. Another student began to talk about his relationship with his father and its effects. Before I knew it, three hours had passed. Now this is a very short version of what occurred and throughout this book, you will feel what I felt that night, but by the end of the night, I watched as eleven men, who had a reason to talk, shared tears and hugs, and "Ah-Hah" moments that made their brotherhood so much closer. That very next week, I shared another story with a virtual stranger. A father who had just moved his son with him came to register his student and spoke with me about his son being a part of the male mentor group, Brother 2 Brother. We happened to be having a meeting that Tuesday and I immediately invited him and his son to join us. As we began our meeting with the traditional; "I Am My Brother's Keeper" and its response, I noticed that the father was intrigued. Now the father and I had spoke a few weeks before this meeting and I began working with his son at this time, but this was the first meeting that the father and son had attended together. So we spent the next two hours talking about upcoming events, the conference we had just attended in Indianapolis, and how we were going to work on our grades and individual GPA goals. Once we ended all of that conversation, the young men came up with a section of the meeting that they like to call, the "Keeping it REAL" time slot. This is the time that the student leaders of the organization get to facilitate the meeting and be their brothers' keepers. At that time, the father and I stepped out of the room. We were just outside in the hall and were able to hear everything that was being said. The son of this father began to speak and share his story.

He immediately felt comfortable enough with his new brothers that he was able to share how he knew he messed up his ninth grade year. He was able to share how he knew that living with his father was the best thing for him right now, and it was at that moment that I looked at the father in the hall with me. The tall, stout man that stood in front of me had begun to cry. This father felt it necessary to apologize to me for crying. I made sure that he understood that this was the power of what we do and that crying is okay. He looked at me and thanked me for this and it was at that moment that I enjoyed another "Ah-Hah" moment!

That same week, my family went to dinner with my father. As we sat having dinner, my father, who has been very supportive of my work and the young people that I work with, asked me about the conference. I went on to share many of the stories from the conference. I also decided to share with him the story about the father and son at our after school meeting. What happened while telling the stories is what helped me to understand the power in the work that had been done. I found myself getting excited as I told the stories for a third or fourth time. I couldn't wait to tell him all of the amazing moments that we had. As I watched the crowd that was around, I started to wonder if they were staring at me wondering what was going on or why is he crying. Again, more tears. Now I started to believe that something was wrong because I had endured more tears in just a matter of days then I care to go through. My wife was not a help to the situation either, because she then begun to cry and again stated how I need to put these stories into a book. I began to believe her. I started to see the light. My father stated that he could see how emotional I was as I told my stories. Maybe someone would read this book. As the old saying goes, the straw that broke the camel's back was that very next weekend when my family went to spend time at my brother-in-law's.

Now my brother-in-law is the definition of the family's keeper. He makes sure that we always get time together. He is the family outing, party, holiday, sporting event, just because gathering guru of the world. We headed to his house on a Friday evening, and it just so happened to be Spring Break. Of course, during the ride, my wife began talking to me about sharing my stories. Once we got to the house, I was able to get around that for the night, but on Saturday morning it came back around in the form of Saturday morning breakfast conversation. I again began telling the stories of the past weekend and also during the week. I shared how this meant so much to all involved and how I hoped that I could continue to involve more students. I shared with my brother and sister-in-law how I was hoping to replicate this same type of work for my young women as well. We talked about that moment in room 408, and how we had that same moment a few days later at our after school meeting. We talked about how these students need to know that they are cared for. How some of these students don't have someone to simply ask them; "How was your day at school?" or "What did you learn today?" A good friend of mine calls me Reverend Strother, because once I get to talking, especially about something that I am passionate about, I don't stop. I am positive that about 15-20 minutes had passed and my zone began to slow down and I looked over at my brother-in-law and wouldn't you know it, HE's CRYING! Again, more tears. My brother-in-law, with all of his knowledge and many times knowledge that he likes to share, just looked at me, stuck out his hand, shook my hand, and gave me that nod of approval. WOW! I knew at that moment that I had to share my stories. I knew that just telling these stories and sharing the experience wouldn't be enough.

I knew that I wanted this to be more than just a book that someone read and either passed onto the next friend or put it in the library to forget it was there. I wanted this to be a book that would cause debates. I wanted teachers to pick this book to read as a part of their curriculum. I wanted teachers and students alike to learn from this book. I also wanted this to be a book that would allow students, my students, to be able to share their ideas of what makes an outstanding teacher. I wanted this book to be a guide to all of our future educators. I wanted this book to help them decide and answer the question, "Do I want to be a teacher, or do I want to teach?" In much of the work we do in school districts, we always attempt to compile a student success team, or student advisory, so that we can get the student perspective. We use this as a tool for what we want the students to learn. What novels will interest them the most? How can we make this history lesson matter to you? Where I believe we have gone wrong is that we have not allowed students input on one very important piece to this puzzle. What makes a great teacher? This is not just a question for the school newspaper. This is not another page in the school yearbook. This is a question that needs to be crucial to the curriculum instilled in universities' teacher preparation programs. As educators, we fail the very young people that we pledge to work with if we believe that just because a person has gone through a traditional four year teacher preparation program and hand her/him the best outlined curriculum map available, that she/he is going to be a great teacher. TEACHING IS MORE THAN JUST MATH, LANGUAGE ARTS, HISTORY, and SCIENCE. That is why this book has been conceived. I have learned more about how to be a great teacher from my students than any class I have ever taken.

The students I have worked with over the years have given me many of the tools that I use today, by allowing me to make mistakes, by allowing me to be a part of their lives, and by simply being who they are. I listened. I turned off my social norm barometer and accepted the grapes that were in front of me. I once heard a story of how teaching students was nothing like making wine. In short, when making wine, you get to toss the "bad" grapes so you can make the best tasting wine possible. As an educator, we do not get to toss the "bad" grapes, we have to make the best tasting wine possible with the grapes we have, and the difference is that those "bad" grapes still have something to offer the wine, you just have to listen, and they will tell how they can work best for you. In this book, I am outlining the ten most important lessons that I have learned from my students. It's in these lessons that I have been able to achieve at high levels. It's in these lessons that I have been able to push my career to the limits. In this book, I will not only share how I learned this lesson, you will also hear from a few of the students who helped me learn this lesson and how they were able to teach me and in return, we hope they will be able to teach generations of teachers to come. So you say you want to teach; here are ten lessons or ideas that need to be learned and comprehended.

1)   **Be an OPPORTUNITY –** *"If you stay ready, you never have to get ready."*– Will Smith

2)   Be a LEADER –*"If your actions inspire others to dream more, learn more, do more and become more, you are a leader."*– John Quincy Adams

3)   **Be a RELATIONSHIP -***"To be trusted is a greater compliment than to be loved.*" **–** George MacDonald

4)   **Be a MENTOR –***"A mentor is someone who allows you to see the hope inside yourself"* – Oprah Winfrey

5)   **Be a PARENT –** *"He who teaches children learn more than they do"* **–** German Proverb

6)   **Be MOTIVATIONAL –***"We are what we repeatedly do. Excellence, therefore, is not an act but a habit."* **–** Aristotle

7)   **Be INSPIRATIONAL –** *"Try not to become a man of success but a man of value."* – Albert Einstein

8)   **Be INVOLVED –***"Service to others is the rent you pay for your room here on earth."* -Mohammed Ali

9) **Be a TEACHER –***"The function of education is to teach one to think intensively and to think critically. Intelligence plus character - that is the goal of true education."* – Dr. MLK, Jr.

10) **Be a STUDENT –***"Get over the idea that only children should spend their time in study. Be a student so long as you still have something to learn, and this will mean all your life."* -Henry L. Doherty

I have spent much of my career listening to all of the different ideas that others cared to share. I learned from some and others I felt were unusable. Many of the lessons that I learned came from students who were oblivious to how much teaching they were doing, and in the beginning, so was I, but teaching they were. I share these lessons for the same reason I teach, because I hope that someone or two will learn. Learn from my lessons and listen to my students…

Chapter 3

Be an OPPORTUNITY

OPPORTUNITY defined: A good chance for *Advancement* or *Progress*

"If you stay ready, you never have to get ready." – Will Smith

I returned home in 2007 to become an administrator at the same high school I attended and graduated from. I had heard from many family members and friends that there was work that needed to be done and they thought I would be a good fit. I was happy in the current district that I was employed with and didn't really have a reason to move on, other than to advance my career. I was approached by a couple of current administrators in my home district asking me if I was interested in coming back to my home school. I had many conversations with my wife, mother and father, current superintendent, and myself. By the end of these conversations, I had come back home hoping to make some type of a difference, not yet understanding the challenge that had been put in front of me.

As I prepared for my return home, I began to study the curriculum, discipline, and the colleagues that I would be working with. I questioned policies, and questioned goals. I enjoyed the new challenge. My home school was not at the level the district or community wanted it to be. I found myself becoming overexcited and I began to feel anxious about what I thought was going to be an easy fix. Let's just make this change and that change. We can move a few people around, get the students under control, then I would be able to wipe my hands and the school would be better. I found out very quickly that this was not going to be the case. There was a lot of work that was going to have to be done, but there were some really exciting things happening that gave us hope. School started to move very fast. I felt like I was hitting the alarm, going to school, finish the day, went home to eat and sleep and it was time to do it all over again. It was not supposed to be this way. I was going to be a part of the team that was going to make things right. How dare these students not cooperate with my plan? Just walk down the hall, on the right side so traffic moves freely and get to class on time. Sounds so easy, but the reality was they were not going to just walk on the right side of the hall. They were not going to just go to class on time because Mr. Strother said so, and there was one particular student who fought me on every idea I had.

If I told this young man to get to class, he went the other way. If I told this student to stop cursing, he would be in my office minutes later for cursing out a teacher. I did not understand how I had been able to reach every other student I had come in contact with. My track record was strong, but this young man was ready to change the way the wind blew. At home, my wife and kids were starting to feel my pressure. I was not the same daddy, husband, or friend. "You have to breathe and think about it," my wife would say. "You have done this before. You have had difficult students, and you got them. You will get him too!" All the words you want to hear when you are struggling. I just could not hear what she was saying at the time. All I heard from her was this; "Breathe... struggle... and ... difficult." That's all I felt at that time and there was really nothing anyone could say or do. Having someone to encourage you is half the battle; the other half has to come from within you. I had to ask myself whether or not I was ready to be done, or was I ready to get this young man on track.

OPPORTUNITY # 1 – Build the relationship!

I know this young man came to my office his freshman year over thirty times. I would come to work and look in my box to get all of the discipline referrals I had for the day, which at the time were averaging about 45-60, and without a doubt, his name would be on one. Depending on the day, he may have multiple referrals. I would sit down in my chair, rock back and begin to read what had occurred. Deep breathe after deep breath. Thoughts of, "What the hell is wrong with this boy!" would run through my head. I finished my initial reading and set the referral down. I picked it back up about 2 minutes later and read it again. Thoughts continued to run through my head, "What the HELL is wrong with this boy!!"

The frustration by November was overwhelming. I began to question whether or not I could reach this young man. Make no mistakes, I knew that we couldn't get them all, but I was determined. Winter break came around and this was my opportunity to get a new game plan assembled. How am I going to get this young man on board? I was not going to let him win. Little did I know, or even understand, it was not my decision whether he allowed me in. We came back from Winter break and started playing the same game. Nothing was different, so I thought. I began to see this young man more. I began having more and more meetings with his mother. I spoke with his dad who lived in another state and it got to the point that his dad was ready to move him to his home and pull him out of our school. At that point I began to really get mean because I felt like I had failed. I was upset with my efforts. I started to direct my attention to other students and eventually succumb to tactics. I continued to have my talks with him and would check on him here and there, but I was really getting dedicated to the male mentor program that a few colleagues and I brought to the area. It was at that time that I attempted to get him involved, but he was not willing to participate. He didn't need to be a part of this group; he had his time with Mr. Strother whenever he had a referral. The light bulb went on when he said those exact words to me. "I don't need to be a part of your group. I see you and hear you everyday anyway." Instantly, the light switch turned on and what he had been trying to tell me all year made sense. This young man wanted to be sent to my office. He wanted to continue to hear my speeches. My office was his outlet. My office was his comfort zone because he knew that inside those four walls, someone cared.

This young man knew that no matter how many times he got a referral, I was going to tell him that he could do better. He knew that I would continue to tell him that he was better than what he showed. This young man knew that he could call me all the names in the book, walk out of my office and the next day I wasn't going to write him off. He knew that the next day Mr. Strother was going to say, "Are you good now? You got that out, so can we go and have a conversation now?" "You cursing at me or acting like you are so tough that I need to be shaking, is not going to stop me from working with you. Eventually you will allow me to help you." The problem, or what I thought was the problem, was that the summer was just around the corner and I was not going to have the time I needed to get to this young man. He was going to be out of my reach and I was going to have to do this battle all over again next year. My only hope was that I now thought I had him figured out. Nonetheless, this young man provided me with another opportunity that I was not expecting… he let me in. He established the relationship that I thought I was not getting.

OPPORTUNITY #2 – Accept what you're given and move fast.

Registration usually falls the first week of August. We were making it through the second day of registration, when this young man and his mother showed up to register. My initial thoughts were, "Uh-Oh. How is this going to play out?" I sat at the registration desk going from student to student, constantly looking back to see how much time I had. The anticipation was as great as waiting for the new roller coaster at Great America. Time seems to move slowly, but with certainty, he and his mother were coming and I am going to have to be two steps ahead. The last student before him was in front of me, and subconsciously, I am sure I took just a little bit longer getting this student all of his/her paperwork. It was like a game of hide-and-go seek once he and his mother were standing in front of me. "Hey Strothers" he said. "How are you doing, sir?" Where was this going? He seems pleasant. Should I be scared? Should I worry? Am I way over-thinking this interaction and my moments of crazy are beginning to rear their ugly head? No! I am not crazy. Something is definitely…different." I want to be in your program." As I looked up from the table, I began to react in that really weird Scooby Doo voice, but as I stated, act fast. "Okay." I started going through the program guidelines and my expectations, all while anticipating him cutting me off. He didn't. He listened. I asked him if he had a shirt and tie, which was part of the requirement. I asked if he was ready for what this commitment meant. I stated the importance of getting good grades, and slowly moved into talking about his past behavior and how that would need to change. This young man did not flinch. "I have to do better Strothers, so I need you to stay on top of me. I want to do everything. If I stay busy, I won't think about that other stuff."

I accepted what I was given and moved on it. I invited him to come and help with freshmen orientation. This would be his first event with the group and I wanted to see how he would respond. Freshmen orientation came around and he was there early. He stepped right in and almost took over. He attached himself to every move I made. I continued to wonder why the change all of sudden and I wanted to know the answer to that question more than you know. I was convinced for a while that he had a bigger plan that I did not want to be a part of. His attachment to me did not just end that night. He began to come to me about his academics. He began to call me more. He wanted to meet everyone he could. A great friend, irreplaceable colleague, and inspirational mentor of mine was on my mind to bring to Kankakee to meet and speak to my students. I had just completed the training to become a Freedom Writer Teacher, which is part of the Freedom Writer Foundation that was founded by the teacher who inspired the movie "Freedom Writer's." Erin Gruwell has provided me with many moments of clarity and I knew she would have a huge impact on all of the young men that I worked with if I could get her to Kankakee, Illinois. We were able to make this a reality in the fall of 2008. I remember Erin and her assistant showing up at Kankakee Community College. We walked through the doors of where the young men were and Erin greeted all the participants with her glowing smile and infectious hugs. I was anticipating this young man to be moved, but what happened at the moment he stood face to face with Erin Gruwell was a Kodak moment. This young man, with all of his cursing out of teachers, fighting, shields upon shields that he had built, looked into the eyes of Erin and began to cry. The moment shared was timeless. He spent the rest of the night by her side.

At the end of the night, this young man came to me and simply stated, "You don't know how much this means to me. It's like you brought a movie star to Kankakee." All I could do was tell him, "You're welcome." I told him to get ready because we had more to come and he again made sure that he told me that he wanted to do everything. Over the next few months, I watched as this young man did a complete 180-degree turn. I watched him work diligently to earn the right to go to Indiana State University to present at a conference. I watched this young man sell pizza cards, so he could earn his way to Stony Brook, New York for the national SAAB (Student African American Brotherhood) conference. It was at this conference that I continued to watch this young man grow. He made sure that Dr. Tyrone Bledsoe, the founder of SAAB, understood that one day, he planned to work for him. He wanted to experience every opportunity that he could and he made the best of that. It was in that moment, in Stony Brook, New York, that I understood what I was doing for this young man. I was providing him with the opportunity to grow. It was in that moment that I knew the importance of providing opportunities for my students. Erin was able to reach so many students through the opportunities that were given. The trips to five star restaurants were special, but not as special as knowing that someone was willing to give them the opportunity. The trips to New York and Indiana meant everything, but it was in his words that I knew that it meant more to him to have been given the opportunity. What is even more exciting is watching the turn that he has made on a personal level, the changes he made for himself. He began to attend and become more involved with his church. He had become so dedicated to church that he even walked to church on Sunday mornings.

His academics grew enormously. Freshman year was not as academically sound as we would have liked it to be. After deciding to join Brother 2 Brother he became a B and C student, even making the B honor roll at one point. I watched this young man become a pillar of our community and our school. I was convinced that it was my mouth and lectures that made this happen. However, what I learned was my conversations with him were vital, but most important were providing the opportunities for change. I provided him the opportunity to be a member of

Brother 2 Brother. I provided him the opportunity to go to Indiana and New York. I provided him the opportunity to speak in front of people about a program that he is so proud of. I provided him the opportunity to turn his grades around. I provided him the opportunity to meet people he felt he would never meet…and he ran with those opportunities and is still running. When we first began our journey together, I told him that if he let me, I would do everything I could to make sure that he would succeed. As it has turned out, I was not the only one providing the opportunity to succeed. What this young man provided me with was the opportunity to believe in what I do. He provided me the opportunity to better my craft. If it had not been for this young man, during the summer months, deciding that he was going to allow me to help him, I was ready to give up. He helped me understand that all things that are good come with time and that in the moments of despair; you have to keep fighting for what's right. This young man gave me the opportunity to be a better teacher. "I knew that this young man was going to go to jail or die, until you got a hold of him Mr. Strother", is what I was told by a good friend of mine. The first time I heard that I thought, well, we did have to work at it. Then I realized that I gave myself too much credit. The decision to change ultimately came from him.

I provide "Nuggets of HOPE", and all I can hope is that they decide to take a bite. If they take one bite, I can get them to take two, but ultimately, the decision to take that first bite…is theirs!

Student Lesson #1- Find Out Who They Are!

Mr. Strother, you are my favorite teacher, and most likely always will be. Even though it was nearly 6 years ago that I had you as my teacher, I still remember every minute of it. You cared about me as a person and tried to help me through my loss. Usually, I would never talk to my teacher about something so personal, but Mr. Strother was different. I knew I could trust him and I wasn't afraid to cry or laugh in front of him. He helped me cope with the loss of my brother. He had passed away when I was in 5th grade and it was the hardest thing I had to deal with. Even though I didn't have Mr. Strother until 6th grade, the emptiness was still in my heart. I needed people to care, and Mr. Strother did just that. He had suffered with many losses himself and knew what I was going through. The comfort he gave me made me feel better and I always knew he was there to talk whenever I needed him.   Also, he would never judge me if I made a little mistake. There was this one specific time I remember when my 2 friends and I had to have a meeting with Mr. Strother. Uh oh, this never happened. We were supposed to be the good kids in class, but one time we made a mistake. My friends and I, I guess you would say, weren't the nicest at the time. We made fun of this one boy in my class, and made him cry! Nobody ever thought that this would happen, so Mr. Strother had a little talk with us. Yes, it was a serious situation, but he was really understanding about it since he was once a kid too. We made some bad decisions and Mr. Strother wanted to make sure it would never happen again. I would never want to be made fun of, so why would I do it to another one of my classmates?

He made me change as a person and still to this day I think about that. Other teachers, I just go to class everyday, then summer comes, and I forget about them. Mr. Strother, though, made a huge impact on my life; there was no way I could forget. Every time I run into him I get this huge smile on my face and want to tell him everything. While he was working at another School District, I was excited every time we had a volleyball game there. As soon as I got to the school I would look around and try to find him. We would always have a good talk afterwards and he would always ask about my family. That means a lot to me knowing that he cares about how my life is going. Yeah, we would have the occasional "school" talk, but he knows that is what every other teacher talks about, and it's boring. He doesn't nag me to death about my grades or tell me what to do because he knows what I am capable of doing. In the classroom Mr. Strother was also very strict. It was a good thing for someone to keep us wild 6th graders in line. We would get out of hand sometimes with our talking and acting up, so he decided to take away all of our desks. We were to set our seats up in a circle around the room. At first nobody liked it and complained, but Mr. Strother stayed with it. Eventually after all the childish whining, we became a family. Everyone could work with each other and had more respect for the teacher. I really don't know how he accomplished this, but Mr. Strother has his ways. Whenever he wants to achieve a goal, he works to his fullest ability until he is able to succeed.

Chapter 4

Be a LEADER

"If your actions inspire others to dream more, learn more, do more and become more, you are a leader."– John Quincy Adams

We have all known or heard the stories of many great leaders. We have watched it in our own homes and communities, but to lead a group of students is a much more daunting task. I once read a short story from an unknown author that told the story of leading troops in battle, but I was able to equate it to a teacher leading his or her students. It read like this:

"I submit to you that leaders will never be more or less than their soldier's evaluation of them. This is the true efficiency report. From most of your troops you can expect courage to match your courage, guts to match your guts, endurance to match your endurance, motivation to match your motivation, esprit to match your esprit, a desire for achievement to match your desire for achievement. You can expect a love of God, a love of country, and a love of duty. They won't mind the heat if you sweat with them, and they won't mind the cold of you shiver with them. You see, you don't accept the troops; they were there first. THEY ACCEPT YOU. And when they do, you'll know. They won't beat drums, wave flags, or carry you off the drill field on their shoulders, but you'll know. You see, living your orders will appoint you to command. No orders, letters, no insignia of rank can appoint you as a leader.

Leadership is an intangible thing. Leadership is developed within yourselves, and you'll get stronger as you go."

Replacing words like "troops" or "soldiers" for words like "students" or "staff" and expecting a love for learning, a love for your school, and a love for your community, makes this story blend well with the life of any teacher. As I read this, I was reminded of a saying that comes from many teachers today, and it just does not mean anything to most students, "Because I'm the teacher." Believing that a student is going to respond to you simply because of your title is one of the biggest mistakes a teacher can make. Your "insignia" does not matter. To truly step into the role of a leader, you have to be ready and prepared to go through the trenches with your students. Standing in front of them and expecting a response "because you're the teacher" will set you up for failure. Be willing to step out and be a unique leader. Do things that no teacher has been willing to do. Dream out loud. Donald Trump once said, "You have to think anyway, so why not think BIG!" Make your dreams bigger than your memories and use those big dreams to challenge your students. As I move forward in my goals with my students, I am always trying to give them the best that I can offer. I don't want them to learn about the Holocaust through a book, I want them to meet a Holocaust survivor and then take them to Germany to see the concentration camps. Stop doing what every teacher has done for the last 50 years. As a teacher, you will be able to earn the respect of your "troops" when they know that you are in control and will make sure that they will be successful, even if it means doing something different.

To be a great leader, you have to be enthusiastic about your career. A great leader has a passion that defies logic. That passion works like a magnet and it draws your students into your world. Don't be worried about what the teachers in the teacher's lounge are thinking of you. The more conversation that is spent on you and how you are working, the more testimony they are giving to your great work. The last great piece to a great leader is an even better vision. Theodore Hesburgh once stated; *"The very essence of leadership is you have a vision. It's got to be a vision you articulate clearly and forcefully on every occasion. You can't blow an uncertain trumpet."* This is a powerful statement. Uncertainty in who you are, and what it is that you plan to achieve will be the death of your passion. Believe in what you want to achieve. I challenge you to not want to be a teacher that just teaches a subject matter. I challenge you to want to change the world. If enough people work hard enough to change the world for the positive, imagine what our world could be like. Do the same with education. If something feels like it doesn't fit, then _say_ it doesn't fit. Be ready to sound your trumpet of certainty. Be a smart leader and know that listening to the other side and trying to comprehend it is just as important as giving your side, but be passionate in your fight. Student growth is not simplistic enough to quantify it to subject matter. As a teacher, you are raising the next generation. I encourage you to have only 1 limit as you work with students, and that is "No Limit."

Chapter 5

Be a RELATIONSHIP

"To be trusted is a greater compliment than to be loved." – George MacDonald

Student Lesson #2 – It's Not About Friendships; It's About Relationships!

I have always had the view, that in order for something large to be successful, the smaller and simpler components of that entity must be the strongest. A well built building, the great pyramids of Egypt, and the infrastructures of awesome civilizations have one thing in common, and that is the fact that in order for them to function properly or even exist it is not the top; but, the bottom, or foundation that is the most supported. If it were not for that fact, all of these great things would crumble to rubble at the first sign of stress. Why then can we not apply the same idea to the success of the world? Countries are the foundation of our world; people are the foundation of our countries; and education is the foundation of any individual person. When broken down this way, one could see that education is the foundation of which the entirety of the world rests upon. Also when broken down this way, it is easy to see why the world is as unstable and feeble as it is and why it suffers greatly from minor problems the way that it does. Education has been a hurdle that America has been unable to jump for decades. Why is that? The U.S. federal government focuses heavily on the education budget; however, is that where our attention should really be placed if we are looking for a solution? Is money the foundation of the educational system? Or could it possibly be something else? As a student currently enrolled in college I feel the answer is a bit more obvious to me seeing that my vision hasn't been tainted with years away from the educational system, and the answer is actually much simpler than monetary increases. The foundation to education is a relationship.

I have witnessed first hand the power that a true relationship between teacher and student can have on the quality of education received, and it is truly amazing the difference that it makes. I can honestly say that Marcus Strother was one of the greatest educators that I could possibly ever have the honor of learning from. Not because of his wealth of knowledge, but because he is one of the few teachers that actually understands what is needed in order for education to occur. In the short time of knowing him we developed a bond that is stronger than any that I have ever had with anyone else. Even stronger than what I have with my own father. I believe that it is because of this; that I actually wanted to learn anything that he had to teach me. When you create a bond with a student you are no longer looked at as a teacher or superior. You are looked at as a very well respected friend. It is a well-known fact that a student would rather take the advice of a peer over the advice of a teacher any day. What educators fail to realize is that students connect more with peers not because of the age similarities but because of the relationship they have with their peers. They spend time together making them the more trustworthy person in their eyes. Because of the strong relationship between Strother and myself, I would find myself going out and seeking information from him, rather than him having to force information onto me. And the passing of information extended way past just educational purposes. If I had a problem in my life he would be the first person I turned to for advice because I knew that he was a friend and that he would be there for me had I ever needed him. For this, I came to truly love him for all that he had to offer and more. There was a point not too long ago when our school district needed to make budget cuts and Strother was on the chopping block.

Because of the relationships that he had with me and countless other students, I used my status as student council president to fight relentlessly for the retention of his position at the school, and a majority, if not all of the student body backed it. It was the greatest organized student effort that I had ever seen personally in my lifetime and it wasn't something that we had to do; however, something that we wanted to do to save someone who we believed in and believed in us. Remembering back, it was a very time sensitive situation because we found out what was going on the day of the board meeting that was to decide his fate and we didn't have much time to come up with a game plan if we were to save his job. I started a petition and the response was incredible. We had an astounding 570 students sign the petition within the first 25 minutes; that was approximately a quarter of our school population. When students have a relationship with an educator like this, they know that it is their education on the line if something were to happen to change that and will actually do anything to keep it intact. I have also seen how important a relationship is from the educator aspect as well. I love kids and when I first arrived at DePaul University I was employed by an organization called Jumpstart. Jumpstart is an organization where college students mentor 3-5 year olds in literacy and social skills to prepare them for their educational career. Of course they had a pre-school teacher; however, it wasn't until me and my fellow jumpstart team members came into the classroom and built our relationships with them that they actually learned to write their names and learn to read. I was amazed to see that even at this young age students responded so much better to someone they had a close relationship with than someone they didn't. There was a certain child in the classroom and for the sake of privacy, let's call him Calvin.

Calvin absolutely hated books. He wouldn't even hold one if you asked him to. Every day during reading I would read to Calvin and he would not even pay attention. He would either run away or throw the book. One day during reading time I told Calvin that we would not be reading but just talking. We talked about things that he enjoyed and simply had a conversation. Laughs were shared and Calvin grew comfortable. After about 2 weeks of this when it came time to read, Calvin surprised me with a book "ChickaChicka ABC". He held out the book and asked "Will you read this to me?" That was a very powerful moment. That was the moment when Calvin no longer saw me as a teacher and began to see me as a friend. By the end of the year Calvin was the one reading books to me and at a mere 3 years of age. After that I knew that education would never be about the money or the expensive equipment. It's about the passing of information from friend to friend. There was once an ancient Chinese saying that was brought to my attention. "There was once a blacksmith who lost a nail. For loss of the missing nail he could not make the horseshoe. For loss of the horseshoe, there was the lack of a horse. For loss of a horse, the message could not be delivered. For loss of a message, the war was lost." For how long are we going to go without that missing nail? For how long are we going to be losing this war in education? And for how long are we going to leave the world unchanged? I have come up with my own saying. For loss of a relationship, the education was never effective. For loss of an education, the people never contributed to society. For loss of a contribution, the countries failed. And for loss of successful countries, our world crumbled. I say, let us save our world from crumbling.

Friendships VS. Relationships

In my first year in administration, I worked with a wonderful woman as my administrative assistant. Her ability to relate to the students, parents, and teachers was like watching an eagle soar through the sky. It was almost effortless. She made working with her so easy, but I was even more excited about what stuck out the most and that was how much I learned from her. She actually coined one of my most favorite phrases; "It's not about FRIENDSHIPS, it's about RELATIONSHIPS!" When I first heard her say this, it stopped me in my tracks because it instantly made an impact. It was so true! At that moment, I took that on as my motto and have not faded from that. I continuously remind myself, even when I think that I cannot work with a student; "It's not about FRIENDSHIPS, it's about RELATIONSHIPS!" Now what exactly does this statement mean? I plan on sharing so much more in this book, but none will mean more to you than this. Taking the time to know a student in their entirety is the single most important factor to being a teacher. There is no secret ingredient to being a great teacher; the only ingredient is to care purposefully. In the process of you caring purposefully for your students, relationships begin to build. Students will know if all you care about is whether or not they understand how to inference a picture or certain passage from a book. They will know if you consider yourself the most important person in the classroom. In building a relationship with your students, they will begin to accept you as a meaningful part of their life. Any person that goes into this profession believing that the student will do what you need them to do just because you have the title of teacher, has already started two steps back instead of front.

I encourage you to hang this in your mind's Post-It notes; "Students want to be lead, but they will not follow you until they believe that you will do everything you can to protect them." Building the relationship is vital. As you move into the career of teaching, you need to ask yourself honest questions about what students you want to work with. Do you want to work with a more at-risk type of student? Do you want to work in a more diverse culture? Are you more comfortable with students who may have the same background as you? Be deliberate with these questions because the answers will guide you to what may be the most effective job placement. What if you don't get a job where you are comfortable? What happens when you are around a culture or environment that you are not accustomed to? Being willing to admit this is step one. "We can't teach what we don't know" is one of the most intriguing book titles, and one of my favorite reads. When placed in an uncertain situation, you must first be able to be honest with yourself and say, "I don't know…" Being placed in a position that is uncomfortable is a strong possibility, so being prepared for that is important. Having that dream job fall in your lap is a possibility as well, and even with that, it is imperative that you find a way to build relationships with your students. Let's look at how you can build those relationships. Whenever you are approaching a new student, or classroom, the little things that you do in the beginning will mean so much. Learning your students' names. Not using the excuse that you are terrible with names. Students find value in their teacher or administrator caring enough to know their names. Practice at home; look over your seating chart. When you're in front of your class, calling on students to participate will help you. Stop standing and lecturing, but take the time to get them involved.

Challenge yourself in front of the class. "I will have your names down within two weeks. If I don't, pizza party on me!" Don't do a challenge that is going to cost you a lot of money, but make the challenge worth it to you. Saving money is a good reason to learn those names. Many teachers use worksheets that they may call the "getting to know you" worksheet. There are a couple of problems with these types of worksheets. One, you are not giving the students enough credit to know that you aren't truly trying to get to know them. This worksheet is really just a fable attempt at you trying to get more information on how to get in touch with their parents if you need to. They realize this. It is at this moment that they are questioning your integrity. They are questioning why you are here. Instead of or as well as doing the worksheet, why not have a class discussion that also involves the students getting to know a little about who you are. Share stories about who you are. I know that much of what I am telling you goes against everything that you are taught in your college courses, but it is those same college courses that aren't preparing our teachers for the real world of teaching. The second issue is that many times these sheets set teachers up for failure. We ask the students questions about themselves, and we may seem interested that day in what they wrote, but do we ever go back and ask questions to the students about what they wrote. "Hey, at the beginning of the year, you wrote that you didn't like Math at all. Has that changed for you? Is there a way that I can help?" Do you share the information that you get with other teachers? If the students tell you that their favorite subject is Science and you teach Language Arts, do you share that information with the Science teacher? Why do we only do the "getting to know you" worksheet at the beginning of the year? Don't things change throughout the semester or year? Should we be more deliberate in what we are doing when we attempt to make a student believe that we want to get to know you? Don't be afraid to get too close. I have been told that I am too close to the students. Being too close to my students helped save my job. My students stood up for me in a way that humbled me for life. My students knew that I was there for them, which many adults have forgotten. We are here for the students. Don't let one bad day or school year for that matter change your mind from that knowledge. As my students refused to go to class, got over 500 names on a petition in less than a half an hour, did a march down the main street of our city at seven in the morning, spoke at numerous school board meetings on my behalf, I knew that I would never allow someone to tell me that I am too close to my students again. They made it known that they wanted me to continue in my position because I cared about them and the school. Again, no secret ingredient, I just cared about them and I showed it. Building relationships can lead you into a position of friendship one day, but isn't that true with all relationships. We all start out as not having a relationship or friendship, and it is taking the time to get to know a person that helps us form those relationships. Once the relationship is formed, we can now start building trust, we can now starting learning how someone functions, build a level of respect, and get to know their likes and dislikes. We learn what is important to them. The students that we are a part of are with us more than they are with their own families. How can you do this job and not feel like you need to gain trust, earn respect, know their likes and dislikes, and what is important to them? The students who are considered "at-risk," to the students who are considered the "honor roll" kids, all want to be cared for.

All students want to know that someone is listening to them and not just counting them out because they are children. Hear what is being said to you, even when no words are coming out of their mouths. Stop running from the non-traditional way of teaching because we can no longer whip out the rulers, snap our fingers, and watch them perform. If you think you are doing a lot to build the relationship, do more. Just simply do more, because our students and our society deserve it!

Chapter 6

Be a MENTOR

"A mentor is someone who allows you to see the hope inside yourself" – Oprah Winfrey

It took many years for me to realize what it meant to be a mentor. When I did realize the idea of being a mentor, it captured my interest beyond belief. I could not wait for the opportunity to give someone a new opportunity that may help him or her realize the potential inside. I began to look at my career of teaching as more of a career of mentoring. How can I help someone realize she can do Algebraic equations? How can I help someone know that college is an option, despite what the research shows? Later in my career, I was able to tell myself that I am not going to get my students to learn anything if I cannot get them to see that they have the potential to change the world. In the world of teaching, you will become a mentor to many students. You will become the one that makes them feel like they can change the world. You will become the light that turns on for them and it is up to you to decide if you are going to make that happen. At the moment a student enters your classroom or office door, there is an awkward moment of silence that you and the student know is there, but it is so quick, you are unable to appreciate it. That moment of silence is something I like to call "THE CLARITY PING!" It is at that moment that you will become the person who makes or breaks the student's day. That moment can change a student's entire outlook on how he approaches education for the rest of his life. How many parents do you know hate school because of their bad experiences? It is 20 years later, and they are still holding onto that moment that made them hate school. There is an upside to this as well, but that depends on the person. I had "THE CLARITY PING" and it is what made me decide to teach. My sixth grade teacher asked me this one question, in her "getting to know you" exercise. "What's it like having a white mother and being black?"

She had not taken her PING and made it work for her. She did the complete opposite, but I turned that negative moment into a drive. I knew that I did not want any other student to ever have to deal with a teacher asking that type of question. What will you do with your "CLARITY PING?" **Teaching is Mentoring!** As someone who teaches, you are getting students to see hope within them, but there is a secret part of mentoring that many people aren't ready to accept and that is, mentoring means having a second family. Mentoring students means long days and nights. Mentoring students means making opportunities for them that they have never experienced before. Mentoring means being there for a student when no one else is. Mentoring means taking the place of someone. As you begin this career of teaching, try to remember who it was that made a difference with you and how did this person make that difference. This person took on the role of mentor. Students are in need of that other figure, that person that doesn't only want to teach them Math and Language Arts. Many of our males need to have that male figure in their lives to help them find the potential within themselves. Many of our females need that same support. That person who is going to listen to them talk about subjects they feel mom and dad just might not get. Be prepared for this because sometimes these conversations will go deeper than you may expect. Being that mentor who can have those conversations, teach them which way to go and the possibilities that are available, is priceless.

Chapter 7

Be a PARENT

"He who teaches children learn more than they do" – German Proverb

Student Lesson #3 - Be more than "Just the Teacher!"

On so many occasions, I have come across peers that describe their home life as nothing more than terrible. They begin to share stories of how they have to wake up in the morning without a mother or father present, and in some cases, no one there to comfort or encourage them at all. Sadly, this is an all too common story for children living in my city. Children in my city face many problems while trying to grow and become young men and women. Often times they have to overcome gang violence, teenage pregnancy, and broken families. I once read in a book that a child's feelings are just like a sheet of fabric softener, very soft and delicate. This is what I feel that all teachers should remember when working with children. One can imagine what it is like for a child that has to face living in a single parent home. They often lack many things that play a detrimental part in their ultimate success. Many of my peers come to school seeking what they don't have at home and that, simply, is a mother and or father. Teachers need to remember while educating students that a child may not be acting out just because they want to be the class clown, but they simply may be acting out to gain attention. Teachers that have lent an extra hand in my life are typically the ones that went above and beyond their normal duties. They were the ones that filled the shoes of my missing father in my life. When I wake up in the morning I find myself wondering what my life would be like if I was living with my father. Although I will never get the opportunity to answer that question, I do know that as long as I have people in my life that provide that fatherly love, I will be able to overcome any and all obstacles that life may bring while growing and becoming that person that I am destined to become. In the time that I have spent at my high school, I have had teachers that have given me the typical teacher attention.

Teachers that generally do this are the ones that normally come to work only because it is something that they must do in order to be financially stable in their personal lives and not because they want to help a student become well equipped for society and what it has to bring. These are the teachers that didn't expect more of me. The teachers that I am describing are the ones that allowed me to walk into class ten minutes tardy and nothing happened, or the ones that allowed me to slack off in class on a regular basis. The definition of a "good teacher" can be described in various ways, but my definition is simply a teacher that makes me do right when I want to do wrong. If my peers are anything like me, then they also need someone that will constantly tell them that they can do better and failing is not acceptable. For me, more or less, it's about having teachers or someone that has a great influence on me, someone that will set standards for me and break my neck if they aren't being met. This is exactly what my High School Dean of Students, Marcus Strother does. Since the beginning of my freshman year, he has told me that I can do better. When I reached a point in my high school journey that I had failed four out of the seven classes, he pulled me aside everyday and told me, "You have to do better. Failing does not belong in you, and you can do better." The one thing that I will always remember is Mr. Strother pulling me to the side and yelling at me until he turned red in the face. At the time I never understood quite why he was yelling, but now, I know it was merely because he cared. Although Mr. Strother is not a teacher, this is the concept I believe teachers should follow in order to become that parent in a child's life. I know that working with my peers can often become a very challenging and tedious process; however a teacher still needs to remember that their responsibility is to teach children. A teacher must realize that children need the love and support of someone in their lives. Remember that you must push a student to do his or her best. Challenge that student to reach for something higher than just a "D" on their report card. Push them to become that over-achiever that many of them try to strive for. Show them that there is an option, and they don't have to go down the road that their mother or father went down. Teachers should become that challenging authority figure in a student's life. What I mean by this is that a teacher should become the person that questions the grades of a student, question why they come to class ten minutes late everyday, and question why they have been slacking off. This process obviously won't work

for every student that you encounter but, if you have a class of thirty and you are able to become a parent in just five of your student's lives, know that you made a big difference. So many times we are teaching without educating.

In my time teaching, I have discovered a few little gems that have allowed me to be successful in the classroom and as an administrator. As I continue to learn new gems that can be used to my advantage, I continue to learn that no matter how my summer goes, or what new ways I believe that I am going to change some of how I do things, there is always one or two students who need me just a little more than usual. There is always that need for attention that throws me into the world of being someone else's parent. If you are not prepared to start a new family or have a second one, don't teach. If you do this job with fidelity, and mean what you do when you do it, you are going to grow admiration from a student that will look at you as more than a teacher. They will expect to hear from you when they do well on their report cards. They will hope for a granola bar from you because they didn't or couldn't eat at home. They will ask you to give them a secret to doing their homework that you haven't told anyone else, and yes, they will give a hug or two as you go throughout the year. As taboo as this is, many of us have lost touch with being comforting human beings. We have forgotten the meaning behind a simple hand on a shoulder, or a hug from time to time. I encourage you to wait until you know you have built a relationship with a student that is one of understanding, but I want you to understand that it will happen, if you teach with care. Many of the students that I work with today come from all types of homes. They come from well grounded, two parent homes. Some come from well-grounded single parent homes. Then there are those students who are just the opposite. They have two parents in the home, but it is the most dysfunctional situation they can be in. Understanding that a student who **_needs_** you can come from any type of home, is crucial for a teacher. I remember seeing an email once that stated, "you want me to be a social worker, nurse, counselor, etc. and after all of that, you still want me to teach," my answer to this is "YES!" Today our students come to us lacking and striving in areas that some of us just can't understand. As someone who teaches, it is imperative that we be as well rounded in our own learning so that we can comprehend what is going on with our students. They depend on us to be there for them in ways that to some, seems like too much. Reaching and teaching students at their level is difficult, but important. I have walked down many school hallways and have watched as those who teach continue to reach out to students like they were their own. I have seen the difference that it can make in a student, when the one constant in her life makes the next 7 hours of the day seem like the best time of her life.

I have watched as those same people who teach have been hard on those same students for not completing an assignment, or were late to school or class. The common factor in both of these situations was the reaction of the student. The student appreciated the teacher praising what they accomplished or the fact that they gave them a hug this morning and asked, "How are you doing?" The student also appreciated when they had to be told, "failure does not belong on you." "Stop choosing to fail and do better."

It's an amazing site when you see a teacher teaching. When you see a teacher connecting with a student on another level. It's like watching number 23 in the last two minutes of the fourth quarter or hearing the greatest voice you have heard singing the national anthem. When it is working and you see the relationship and how it is changing the student, you see the ray of light and you hear the "AHHHH" sound as it moves through your ears. In a word, it is AMAZING! Open up your heart.

Erin Gruwell is someone I consider a great friend. She is also someone who has mastered building relationships. She wrote a book called, Teach with Your Heart. In this book, Erin lays out how she had to choose the students over the adults. How she chose to teach with her heart. Go with your gut as some would say. Take the time and ask yourself, "If I were my own student, would I like me as a teacher? Would I learn from me? Would I be excited about coming to my class?" If you can't honestly answer, "Yes," to these questions, then reflect on what needs to change. Follow or teach with your heart.

Chapter 8

Be <u>MOTIVATIONAL</u>

"We are what we repeatedly do. Excellence, therefore, is not an act but a habit." –
Aristotle

As we move forward in lessons, the next two are very simple, yet very important. Being motivational and inspirational are strategic to the success of being able to teach. Being motivational means being someone who manifests his or her words into action. It is by creating opportunities for students that you will allow yourself to motivate them into being or seeing the world as a much bigger place than just the neighborhood they grew up in or the corner store down the block from their house. Being inspirational is about learning how to make your words powerful. Motivation = ACTION / Inspiration = Powerful WORDS. Let's continue to talk about how being able to teach means being able to motivate. As you move into your classroom, you will encounter students who just aren't motivated to participate, operate, or generate successful outcomes for themselves. They will be stuck in a world of negativity or unsuccessful ways. It will take new opportunities to get them to reach for success; in order to help them start moving towards the choice of being motivated. Many of the students that you may encounter have been watching failure occur in their life for so long they have or will have forgotten what it feels like to be successful. They will not understand that there is another way of doing things until they are motivated to that choice of life.

Failure is a choice. Remember this motto for as long as you teach, that FAILURE IS A CHOICE! There are no students who don't want to succeed, but there will be those students who don't know how not to fail, so for them, failure is a natural way of life. It's at this moment that you will need to begin to create opportunities for your students to succeed. As their teacher, it will be a part of your teaching to provide motivational tools that will push them into a succeeding way of life. These opportunities can come in a lot of forms. Modified assignments that will allow them the opportunity to do well. It will be at your determination when you begin to lengthen those assignments into a full load of work. Class discussions that relate real world activities to the activities you are doing in your classroom. By doing this it will allow the students the ability to find a common place that is familiar to them. This common place, filled with successful endings, will begin to manifest itself into a normal way of life. This will take time, so being patient is important. Inspirational and motivational speakers coming into your classroom are very intentional efforts as someone who teaches, to bringing a new ideological way of looking at life to your students. The great thing about bringing in different speakers is that you can control what your students are going to hear. Bring in speakers that you have had the pleasure of hearing yourself, or those that have been referred by someone you trust works great as well, but always be sure that you know the message that is going to be brought. In my teaching career, I have had the opportunity to bring speakers into my students' lives that have all had a different message, but was motivational for many different reasons. My students have been able to hear such speakers as Hill Harper, Erin Gruwell, Lasana Hotep, and Dr. Tyrone Bledsoe, just to name a few. Each one of these speakers were able to touch my students by a message that they felt was important to them, so it then became important to my students. Messages that are as wide as staying in school and going to college, to how you can become a change agent for your community, all have played a role in making my efforts even easier, because now the students are beginning to see that there is a bigger world out there and that young people just like them have made a difference.

Another key component to being motivational is providing your students with field trips. I do not mean your typical museum trips, or a trip to the zoo. These are not bad field trips, but they are so taboo, that they have lost their luster for creating a new opportunity that is going to motivate students into a new way of life. I have heard of students not wanting to attend those trips anymore because they are so typical. Reach for the stars with your trips. Erin Gruwell used field trips not only to reward, but to teach. Here is where this gets touchy because we all know that money is scarce in education and it is hard for us to afford the type of trips that I am talking about, but I will give you some ideas for ways to combat that. Finding funds is a much easier task than many make it, but the one component that stops many people from achieving their goal is having the go ahead to ask someone for help. We immediately shut ourselves down because we believe we will be told, "No." Banks are a good source for funding. Many banks are required to give back at least 20 % to their working community each year, therefore, ask them for money. Some department stores offer programs that have very simple ways to get funding. Here is another untold secret that many people don't like to talk about, but it is true. There are philanthropists all over the world that want to help you out, especially if you are working with minority students. Take a small proposal to these philanthropists showcasing the work that you are doing with minority students and ask them for help. Believe it or not, there are many individuals who want to help just for that reason; you are working with minority students. The problem is they don't know what to do to help, therefore, give them a way to help and watch how they come to your aid. There are some great people with money who know that our educational field is suffering. Allow them to help because they want to! Field trips can teach students educationally and motivationally. Create an opportunity for a student in your class, who loves to sing, and loves to dance to attend a Broadway play. This can be a motivational tool that changes that student's entire way of living. Create an opportunity for students to go downtown Chicago and "Skate on State," this type of opportunity can change the culture in which they are adapted. They are able to realize that other minorities' ice skate. That there are minority families that do this as a part of their natural day, and they may also realize that they can do this same exact opportunity for someone else. If you are doing a lesson on the Holocaust, figure out a way to take your students to a tolerance museum, or actually take them to where the concentration camps were. Shoot for the stars, because these are the types of events in someone's life that can change how this person lives. They provide motivation for change. If you cannot make this type of trip happen, then go out and bring a Holocaust survivor into your classroom to speak to your students. Being motivational is about bringing action to your classroom. Teaching them about other cultures, expanding their worldviews, and creating opportunities for change will only guide them in the direction of success. Providing a world where they are motivated by success will be one of the tasks that you will need to master. Create an opportunity and pass on HOPE!

Student Lesson # 4 - Inspirational People

An inspirational person is someone who goes above and beyond in every aspect of his or her lives. An inspirational person loves his/her work with every fiber of his/her being. An inspirational person exerts an energy that makes you want to posses the same qualities. Most of us are familiar with inspirational characters like Martin Luther King Jr., Winston Churchill, Mahatma Gandhi, and Oprah Winfrey. Teachers too, can be an inspiration to their students and co-workers. Since teachers and administrators spend seven to nine hours a day with students, it is important that these professionals positively influence their students. How can I be an inspirational teacher, one might ask? Inspirational teachers know their students, operate with an exceedingly great joy for their work, and are able to create an environment in which the student believes in his or her full potential. It is important teachers place paramount significance on thoroughly understanding their students. It is not sufficient enough that teachers know their student's names and their daily participation level. Teachers must be able to translate actions and words into the deeper feelings a student may have. It may be unorthodox to some to pull a student out of class and say, "What's going on with you?" but these actions are the ones that show students how fervently you care for them. As a student, it's easy to believe the people attempting to teach you everyday are not concerned with you, but more with subject matter. As I am sure most would agree, a young person's education is of the most importance. That being said, never should Mathematics, English or any other subject be placed before a teacher's attempt to ensure the well being of a student. If you want to truly know your students, create activities early in the academic year and throughout to get to know them. Believe it or not, simple games and class discussions give students the platform to share themselves.

Even the most closed students share when comfortable. Class discussions are a particularly good way to learn who students are. For ages of time, conversation has been the pathway to relationship building. This concept is no different in the classroom, on the field, or in the office. Relate the class discussion to the subject matter. By doing this, it will allow students to think and share themselves with you, and you with them, all at the same time. Once a teacher is able to understand the needs, lives, likes and dislikes of individual students, he or she can then begin to educate and more importantly stimulate a yearning for education. Teaching is a gratifying profession. As gratifying as it is, teachers are often plagued with stressors from students, co-workers and personal issues. For some students a teacher is one of the first people seen in the morning. It is imperative that teachers realize this and act accordingly. The mood of a teacher early in the day and throughout plays a colossal role in the experience the student will have at school. Exuding joy and confidence is a contagious action that infects students with immense gratification. When teachers invest their entire spirit in their lesson plans, classroom instruction and interaction with students, it truly shows. Students respect passion and genuine efforts. An inspirational teacher will never submit half efforts or show weariness. The most effective teachers will mystify their students. Students should be left wondering at the ending of every day why their teacher is always so happy. Your joy for teaching may not always be easily read by the student. You can express this joy in several easy ways. When teachers speak, they should speak as if every word is of crucial importance. "Great job!" "How was your weekend?" and "Please read chapter four," should all be delivered with passion in the voice. I am not implying that one should inflate his or her mood. Students do, however, recognize when a teacher is cheerful about what he or she is doing.

In sharing your passion for your profession, it is important to share other things with your students you are passionate about. Your family, friends, hobbies and life stories all assist in helping build an understanding of each other. As you share, students will share, and you will inspire. Inspiring teachers are able to pass on inspirational characteristics to their students. The infectious zeal for education and success being implanted in the students' goal book is the key to being an inspirational teacher. Inspirational teachers want more than to be admired or respected, they should strive to produce respectable, admirable students. People who are able to succeed in business, politics, and in sports are successful not just because of talent. Successful people are successful because they have been able to get others to buy into their vision. You cannot lead a group of people if they do not have faith in the vision. Inspirational teachers can sell that vision. Whatever that vision may be. Once a student believes in your vision, and is able to see him or herself as a successful student, it is at that moment that you have become an effective, inspirational teacher. It is important that your students know a few things about you. Your students should know what your motivations are, why you became a teacher, and how sincerely you truly love your line of work. When students of any age know these things, relationships form. Allowing students to know these things about you removes the clinical-ness of teaching and creates an atmosphere of comfort. Striving to be an inspirational teacher should not be your goal or should such a status be considered a career plateau. Excellence in teaching is a demonstration of the ability to understand your student, the ability to share your love for your career, and the ability to foster students who have a zeal for excellence in their own lives.

If you can accomplish all of these things, and you can, you will prove yourself a truly inspirational teacher. What happens when you know an inspirational character? If you worked with, lived with, and studied with inspiration all around; would that affect your life? One would imagine it would, especially since people we don't know inspire us daily. All of us know, or have known, inspirational people at some point in our lives. Many times I, and I'm sure others, wonder how inspirational people become an inspiration.

Chapter 9

Be INSPIRATIONAL

"Try not to become a man of success but a man of value."– Albert Einstein

The school policy is no hats, headphones, or pajamas at school. As someone who teaches, you are standing in the halls and a student comes walking down that same hall with one of these three things on, if not all of them. Your immediate response is to say, "Take off that hat," or "No pajamas." Immediately, you have started your day in negativity and have now thrown that student into a world of frustration that could lead into a larger issue. Just imagine the difference it would make if you walked up to that same student and greeted him with a "Good morning, love the Cubs hat, but I need you to take it off in the building." Do you think the reaction of the student is going to be different? You have the control as to what your classroom is going to look like day to day. The moment you greet a student, or the first one-on-one conversation you have with that student, or the class discussion you are having, can make or break the students in your class. Your words have more power than you give them credit. Being inspirational is something that you will need to work at doing, but it will need to be a way of life if you choose to be someone who teaches. Recognizing a student's new haircut and making a comment towards that can allow you an opening that you have never had with a student. Another major part of being an inspirational teacher is how you teach. Teaching a lesson is not just about pointing out the facts, it is more about the delivery of the lesson. If a student can feel the passion in your voice for what you are teaching, it will inspire them to want to learn. If you sound like you don't enjoy yourself, then they will also not enjoy themselves. Teaching is like theatre. Imagine going to a musical and the lead singer/actor is fumbling through the words, singing songs as if they wish they did not have to sing them; are you going to enjoy yourself at that musical? Are you going to want to continue viewing that musical? Of course you won't! Now reverse these actions and listen to the singers put passion into telling you how much they love the person they are singing about. Imagine yourself watching them deliver a performance that is making you believe that you are seeing Ray Charles himself, even though you know it is Jamie Foxx. You hold onto every moment. You don't want it to be over because you are enjoying yourself so much. That is what your students should feel every time you teach. Speaking life into Mathematics or Science is an art form. Have you ever watched a great teacher? Have you ever been inspired by someone's word? That's how important you are as someone who teaches. Your words need to inspire great leaders, doctors, future teachers, lawyers, plumbers, website designers, presidents, etc.

As much as we as educators hate for someone to tell us that we may have hurt a student by what we said, we must understand that the words that we deliver are crucial. Creating a culture within your classroom is going to take you inspiring your students into believing in your vision. This has to be a genuine gesture, and without genuine thought going into your work, the inspiration you could inspire will be negative. We miss this important factor when it comes to how we inspire students, because just as we can inspire a student in the positive, we can also inspire them in the negative. Inspirational people are those who keep you hanging onto every word. Inspirational people convince you that you also need to be passionate about what they are talking about. If a person is truly inspiring, then they can lead a group of people into bus boycotts. Can you convince your students that the novel they are about to read is one of the most exciting works of literature they will come across? Can you inspire a multitude of students to believe in what you are saying? As educators, we always say; "If I can reach one student, then I have done my job?" I challenge you to move a nation. Let's change that saying. "If I can reach all students, I can change the world!" Work at changing a multitude of people and stop being satisfied with one. If Martin Luther King, Jr. were happy with getting one person to march with him, would he have made the same difference? Change your classroom, not just one student. Inspire a nation of leaders.

Chapter 10

Be INVOLVED

"Service to others is the rent you pay for your room here on earth." -Mohammed Ali

My wife and I have worked really hard at showing our own children the importance of helping others. We have made our children clean out their rooms of old toys that they don't play with anymore, or clean their closets of clothes that can no longer be worn. We have taken them to churches to wrap gifts for children less fortunate, with the hope that they will continue this habit throughout their life. The ultimate goal for all of this is that they pass it onto their own kids, friends, etc. As educators, we have to understand that we are not only here to teach lessons in subject matters, but also lessons of life skills such as giving and helping others. I always tell the young men and women in my mentor groups that the best way they can repay me for anything that I have done for them is to not pay it back, but to pay it forward. It is easy for us as educators to get caught in the necessity of teaching to the test, or making sure our average grades aren't showing failing grades, but when you choose to be a teacher, you are choosing to teach character. The best educators teach by doing. Don't allow the "system" to scare you away from being a person of humanity. Many educators feel like being humane gets in the way of teaching our young people to be prepared for the real world. This is a sad excuse for educators who believe that their "real" world is the only "real" world anyone should know. I would push upon any educator to ask yourself, "who helped me and how did they do it?" Was there ever a time when I made the wrong choice? Remember... someone went the extra mile for me to help me understand what I did wrong and how I can change my behavior for the next time. This chapter is not about telling educators to give their students money, or to buy them new clothes if they need it. This is not about being a servant leader by making your own family suffer from what you do, although, if one truly cares about what happens to the students they work with, they may spend some money or buy a lunch or two. This chapter of the book is about going that extra mile in ways that aren't typical to what "educators" do. If you believe that in order for you to do bus duty you should get a stipend, don't do this job. Making sure your students get on the bus safely is part of being an educator. Staying after school to work with a struggling student is part of being an educator. Coming to your student's football game to show your support for him, is part of being an educator. The students you work with will look to you for support in areas you couldn't imagine. Taking that extra step to get them on your side will go very far. How many of us truly understand the importance of having a supportive community? There are schools today that are the high achieving schools they are because of the community support they have. This can also affect you being a high achieving educator. If members of your community look at you as a leader in the community, someone who is involved with their community outside of just educating their students, they will begin to work hard for you as parents, community leaders, etc. I worked at a school in a community that was 45 minutes from my home. I was not born or raised in this community, but once I became invested in the community, educating the students became much easier for me. I involved myself in activities throughout the community that allowed for me to build relationships with community stakeholders. This investment paid off, and I still have relationships with many of those students and stakeholders more than five years removed from that community. I would work with community parades, or charity walks that happened in the area. I would participate in summer events that occurred so my old and new students would see me. These small investments in serving the community in which I worked brought me high returns.

I encourage all educators to make these same investments. If your students, as well as community stakeholders see you as just someone who is here to get a check, they will not buy into your vision for their students. Many educators have forgotten that we work for the students. Help the students understand that you are there to serve them. Educate your students on how to use you to the best of their ability. We are the servants and the students are whom we serve. This educational system has found itself in a position where we are no longer here for the students, but here for the adults. Be an educator with a purpose centered completely on benefiting the lives in which you come in contact with. The best educators will become so good at serving students that you will become a servant to students who you don't have a day-to-day contact. This is a great story because the students have now created a culture around you that says you are someone to be trusted. You are someone that the students can depend on and when they believe in you, so will the community stakeholders involved. Build your own personal culture. What happens around you is only what you allow to happen around you and when students understand your own personal culture, they will adapt and educating them will come with ease. That culture is created when students know you are there for them. Students come first!

Chapter 11

Be someone who TEACHES

"The function of education is to teach one to think intensively and to think critically. Intelligence plus character - that is the goal of true education."
– Dr. Martin Luther King Jr.

As I thought about this book and the message I wanted to get across to the reader, it was crucial for me to get people to understand the difference between being a teacher, and someone who teaches. Throughout most of this book, I have attempted to guide those who may already be teaching or are thinking about taking this on as a career, into a place that allows you to understand what this job really entails. Many educators will read this book and disagree with much of what is said, and then there will be those educators who will shake their head in agreement. As much as I hope this book causes many grand discussion groups and debates, I hope that it truly gets people to understand that just because you have gotten a degree in teaching and even landed a job in the field, that those things alone will not make you a teacher. A teacher does not work 8-3, count down Christmas break in September, Spring break during Christmas break, plans their summer vacation right after they return from the last summer vacation, writes 100 referrals a year, calls only the parents that won't argue, and prays for 4 day weekends. Being someone who teaches means "Changing Lives." When teaching is occurring, that person is creating an opportunity and passing on hope. Being someone who teaches means bringing life to the pages of a book by making connections to the students that help them comprehend concepts, sentence patterns, inference, subject to verb agreement, and before a students realizes it, they are 22 stanzas into a poem by Maya Angelou. When someone who teaches is at work, walking a student to the bus becomes a chance to learn just a little more about that student, and not time being taken away from locking up your classroom. When someone who teaches is at work, parents become partners and not that disconnected phone number or dysfunctional parent. When someone who teaches is at work, discussions in the classroom become moments of clarity and not an inappropriate comment or argument. When someone who teaches is at work, grading papers become testimonies of assessment that attest to the job you have done. When someone who teaches is at work, Christmas break becomes a needed time-out to prepare for the next semester and not just another vacation. When someone who teaches is at work, summer break is a long planning period for the next class, not the end to a horrible year. Being a teacher for many is an opportunity to coach football, basketball, softball, etc. That is when you need to ask yourself if you are doing a service or disservice to the students you serve. Is it fair for 150 or 25 students to compromise their education because the students you truly care about are the 10-25 students on your team? Being someone who teaches takes the term "student athlete" for its importance and forces their team to be the student first and the athlete second. Our educational system has been swallowed into a black hole of mediocrity and we have found comfort in this mediocrity. Challenge yourself to be someone who teaches and not just another teacher. Walk proud in this profession. Stop allowing our society to make educators second-class citizens. Teaching someone is crucial to the continued running of our lives, and it is because someone took the time to teach someone else that we have doctors, lawyers, sports agents, nurses, engineers, farmers, marine biologist, etc. If you haven't realized that you are teaching the next generation of teachers, politicians, scientists, and marine biologists, so that our world can continue to function as it does or better, then you won't find purpose in what you are doing. Be someone who teaches, and teach the world.

Chapter 12

Be a STUDENT

"Get over the idea that only children should spend their time in study. Be a student so long as you still have something to learn, and this will mean all your life." -Henry L. Doherty

Within this career, it is known that as an educator you are not going to make a lot of money. There are many educators who understand this and are not doing this job for the monetary finance that is given. If making money is what you are attempting to achieve as a goal, then this section of the book can be simplified by stating that the more degrees you earn, the more money you can make in this profession. I am not attempting to guide you down the path to getting more degrees for the sake of making more money. I am however, attempting to get you to understand the importance of continuous growth in education. A great teacher will learn with her students. The greatest methodology to teaching is to teach by example. Always allow your students the opportunity to see you learning. Many of our students are visual learners and many of our students want to know that they are not being asked to do something that you wouldn't do yourself. Read while they are reading. Have discussions with your students about books that you have read. Share stories of when you were in school that will help them relate to their own experiences. This world is ever changing and because of this, as educators, we have to continue to change. We have to be up on the latest language terms, and understand the new music that is in the air. We have to read the short and the long articles. We have to be able to agree to disagree. We have to learn all of the meanings behind the alphabet soup of education, i.e. PBIS, TAT, RTI, IEP, etc. Even those initiatives that we do not believe are the best; we have to research ways to make them work for your students and work for you.

As I thought about what I wanted to relay to new and veteran teachers through this book, I knew instantly that I wanted to express the need to continue to learn. I knew that I wanted to express to educators to continue to up their level of textual lineage, but I didn't know if this was going to be enough. I had to ask myself; what does it mean to an educator when they continue to learn? What does it mean to a student when his teacher continues to learn? It means that the true definition of education means something to you as an educator. There are 5 different definitions you will find when looking up the word "education" on **www.Dictionary.com**, but let's just look at the first two.

> **1.**The act or process of *__imparting__* or *__acquiring__* general knowledge, developing the powers of reasoning and judgment, and generally of preparing *__oneself__* or *__others__* intellectually for mature life.

> **2.**The act or process of *__imparting__* or *__acquiring__* particular knowledge or skills, as for a profession.

By definition, education needs to occur on two levels. These two levels are simply defined as teacher and student. Being the instructional leader in the classroom, it is the goal of the educator to instill the pedagogy of education into the students that you come in contact with. It is important that we also understand that the learning that will occur in the classroom will not only be the learning that comes from the textbooks or novels that are read. Much of the learning that will occur will come from the personal real life experiences that you and your students have in life. The students come to you with their own cultural beliefs and pedagogies, but it is up to us to allow them to understand that their cultures and beliefs are important, but they are not the only facets of life that they need to understand. The definition reads "the power of reasoning and judgment." If we allow ourselves not to be reasonable in our judgments, then how can we expect to teach them?

As educators, we tend to bring only our cultures and beliefs into the classroom. Then we work very hard to instill those cultures and beliefs into our students, and this is not a bad thing, but we need to also know how to balance the two. Making a student follow your beliefs without accepting that their beliefs are just as important can only taint the potential that they could have. In order for you as an educator to accept the beliefs and cultures of your students, then you have to learn what those cultures and beliefs are. This will again forward you the necessary knowledge to relate to your students and build relationships. Students want lines. They want to know that there are limits to your classroom, and most of all, they want to know that someone cares. I have been involved in education for over 10 years and I have learned many lessons from my students, administrators, fellow teachers, parents, my wife, and my own children. I have been able to learn from others through books, articles, interviews, and discussions. The one and most important lesson I have learned in teaching is that I have to step into this profession with intent. I have to be purposeful in the job that I do. The children that you will work with are in need of a guide. It is your job to challenge them everyday. It is your job to hold them accountable for being successful. It is your job to be someone who teaches.

Chapter 13

"The Response"

"Because I want to coach football!" Yes, it is true that most football coaches are teachers, and yes, many school districts require the football coach to be a teacher, but that should not be why you want to teach. I did a very quick scan in my mind of what my response was going to be and I hoped to not embarrass my nephew in front of his peers, but I found it only fair that I share my thoughts about his decision and explanation on why he wanted to be a teacher. Coaching, whether it is football, basketball, baseball, softball, volleyball, etc. does have its high points in the world of middle / high school competition. Summer's off, winter and Thanksgiving break, and of course Spring break are all attributes to teaching, but they are definitely not or should they ever be, a reason to become a teacher. What is not an attribute to brag about in the education field is that we have "teachers" who are doing this job exactly for those reasons. In other countries, the career of education is veered as one of prestige. The teacher is nothing short of a professional. The teaching profession is equivalent to that of a doctor, lawyer, etc. In our American culture, we have stained the profession of teaching and the educational system as a whole. The elephant in the room that no one wants to admit is that we, educators, have caused most of that stain. There are those teachers who are doing this job because they simply want to coach, enjoy summers off, or want to call themselves a teacher, but many of them don't do the job of teaching. Understanding that there is NO teaching without learning is critical to the profession of teaching. Pablo Freire, one of the most prolific education reformers of our time speaks to this very piece. His words bring an end to the beginning:

"There is, in fact, no teaching without learning. One requires the other. And the subject of each, despite their obvious differences, cannot be educated to the status of object. Whoever teaches learns in the act of teaching, and whoever learns teaches in the act of learning. From the grammatical point of view, the verb to teach is a "transitive-relative" verb, that is, a verb that requires a direct object (something) and an indirect object (someone). In this sense, to teach is teaching something to someone. But to teach is much more than a transitive-relative verb. And this is clear not only from the context of democratic thought in which I place myself but also from an essentially metaphysical point of view in which my comprehension of the cognitive process is grounded. In other words, simply "to teach" is not possible in the context of human historical unfinishedness. Socially and historically, women and men discovered that it was the process of learning that made (and makes) teaching possible. Learning in social contexts through the ages, people discovered that it

was possible to develop ways, paths, and methods of teaching. To learn, then, logically precedes to teach. In other words, to teach is part of the very fabric of learning. This is true to such an extent that I do not hesitate to say that there is no valid teaching from which there does not emerge something learned and through which the learner does not become capable of recreating and remaking what has been thought. In essence, teaching that does not emerge from the experience of learning cannot be learned by anyone."